Lovebirds

A Guide To Keeping Lovebirds

Lovebird Facts & Information, where to buy, health, diet, lifespan, types, breeding, fun facts and more!

By: Lolly Brown

Copyrights and Trademarks

All rights reserved. No part of this book may be reproduced or transformed in any form or by any means, graphic, electronic, or mechanical, including photocopying, recording, taping, or by any information storage retrieval system, without the written permission of the author.

This publication is Copyright ©2019 NRB Publishing, an imprint. Nevada. All products, graphics, publications, software and services mentioned and recommended in this publication are protected by trademarks. In such instance, all trademarks & copyright belong to the respective owners. For information consult www.NRBpublishing.com

Disclaimer and Legal Notice

This product is not legal, medical, or accounting advice and should not be interpreted in that manner. You need to do your own due-diligence to determine if the content of this product is right for you. While every attempt has been made to verify the information shared in this publication, neither the author, neither publisher, nor the affiliates assume any responsibility for errors, omissions or contrary interpretation of the subject matter herein. Any perceived slights to any specific person(s) or organization(s) are purely unintentional.

We have no control over the nature, content and availability of the web sites listed in this book. The inclusion of any web site links does not necessarily imply a recommendation or endorse the views expressed within them. We take no responsibility for, and will not be liable for, the websites being temporarily unavailable or being removed from the internet.

The accuracy and completeness of information provided herein and opinions stated herein are not guaranteed or warranted to produce any particular results, and the advice and strategies, contained herein may not be suitable for every individual. Neither the author nor the publisher shall be liable for any loss incurred as a consequence of the use and application, directly or indirectly, of any information presented in this work. This publication is designed to provide information in regard to the subject matter covered.

Neither the author nor the publisher assume any responsibility for any errors or omissions, nor do they represent or warrant that the ideas, information, actions, plans, suggestions contained in this book is in all cases accurate. It is the reader's responsibility to find advice before putting anything written in this book into practice. The information in this book is not intended to serve as legal, medical, or accounting advice.

Foreword

If you like the bold aura of a parrot but you're not quite certain that you can keep a large size bird, then lovebirds could be a much more suitable pet for you!

Lovebirds are very affectionate to their owners and people in general. They have playful and cheerful personalities and manageable behaviors. They may tend to become mischievous at times and nippy around young children which can pose a somewhat challenging journey but with proper training and guidance, any newbie keepers will surely enjoy taking care of these amazing parakeets. As long as you're willing to learn and willing to be patient, then keeping lovebirds can be one of the best things that can happen to you!

If you want to learn how to keep and raise these beautiful bird species then this book is for you! You'll learn about the biological information of lovebirds, proper husbandry practices, diet and feeding, types of lovebirds, health and medical requirements, breeding basics and other essential information about taking care of these wonderful feathered pets.

Table of Contents

Introduction 1

Chapter One: Basic Biological Information 7

    Appearance 9

    Size 9

    Distribution / Range 10

    Diet and Feeding 10

    Health and Longevity 11

    Behavior and Temperament 12

    Breeding 14

    Fun Facts about Lovebirds 14

Chapter Two: Different Lovebird Species 17

    Peach-faced Lovebird 18

        Peach – Faced Lovebird Specs: 19

    Black - Masked Lovebirds 20

        Black – Masked Lovebird Specs: 21

    Fischer's Lovebird (Agapornis fischeri) 23

        Fisher's Lovebird Specs: 24

    Rare Lovebird Species Found in the Wild 26

    Abyssinian Lovebirds 26

    Lilian's Lovebird 28

        Lilian's Lovebird Characteristics: 29

Threats to Lilian's Lovebird 30

Black - Cheeked Lovebirds (Agapornis nigrigenis) 31

    Black – Cheeked Lovebird Characteristics: 32

Black-collared Lovebirds 32

    Black - Collared Lovebirds Characteristics 33

Grey - Headed Lovebirds (Agapornis canus canus) 34

    Grey - Headed Lovebirds Characteristics 35

    Male Grey – Headed Lovebirds Characteristics: 36

    Female Grey – Headed Lovebirds Characteristics: 36

Red - Faced Lovebird (Agapornis pullarius) 37

    Red - Faced Lovebird Characteristics: 38

Chapter Three: Acquiring, Feeding and Housing Lovebirds
.... 41

Acquiring Lovebirds and Initial Costs in Keeping One ... 42

    Get an Avian Vet 42

    Acquire a Lovebird through Adoption/ Rescue 43

    Acquiring from Breeders and Pet Stores 44

    Basic Needs of Lovebirds 45

First Few Days Home 49

Identification for Your Lovebirds 51

Feeding Your Lovebirds 52

Food for Your Lovebirds 55

Housing Your Lovebirds 57

    Setting Up a Bird Cage 58

    Cage Accessories 61

    Cleaning the Bird Cage Tips 63

Chapter Four: Grooming and Keeping Your Lovebirds Happy 65

    Grooming Your Lovebirds 66

        How to Bathe Your Lovebirds 67

    Trimming Your Bird's Wings 68

    Clipping Your Bird's Nails 70

    Caring for Your Lovebirds' Beak 71

Chapter Five: Handling, Taming, and Training Your Lovebirds 73

    Steps in Handling, Taming and Training Your Lovebirds 74

Chapter Six: Keeping Your Lovebird Healthy 85

    Common Illnesses of Birds 86

        Egg Binding 86

        Respiratory Infection 86

        Heavy Metal Toxicity 87

    How to Tell If Your Lovebird is Sick 88

    Treating Lovebirds 89

Chapter Seven: Basic Breeding Tips 91

    Breeding Your Lovebirds 92

    Materials for Breeding 93

    Glossary of Important Terms 95

Photo Credits 101

References 102

Introduction

Lovebirds are very popular bird species and are good pets for newbie owners. They are great pets for older children but may be a bit too nippy for younger children. Lovebirds may tend to become nippy as they mature if they are not consistently and properly handled. As for most owners, what they do is to keep them with another lovebird so that they won't get lonely. However, it's quite possible that they will form a bond with their own kinds more than you.

Introduction

The most common types of lovebirds that are usually kept as pets are Peach – Faced Lovebirds, Masked Lovebirds, and Fischer's Lovebirds. If this is your first time keeping birds, then it's wise that you purchase a baby bird or a hatchling rather than an older or mature lovebird because baby birds are easier to tame, train, and handle compared to adults. A younger bird usually has a darker shade of black in their beaks compared to older birds. This dark black color in their beaks normally vanishes once they reach four months old. However, it can be vary for different color mutations.

Lovebirds have a scientific name of *Agapornis*, and these birds originated from Africa and Madagascar. There are various types of lovebirds that exist today, and later on in this book you'll see their different characteristics so that you can choose which one best suits you. There are also different colors available for lovebirds, and as a matter of fact, many breeders today have come up with various color mutations.

When it comes to personalities and behaviors, these birds are pretty docile as long as they are raised right. As mentioned earlier, they may tend to get nippy at times but generally speaking, they are not aggressive birds. They can easily bond with other parakeets and their own kinds as well as with people. In general, males are less temperamental compared to female love birds. Females are generally more

Introduction

curious and more playful or energetic than their male counterparts. These birds love to hang out and go inside out huts and boxes or something that they can poke their heads in. This is why it's best that you provide their cage with something like that unless of course it will cause them to become aggressive with other birds. Make sure to provide enough of them to avoid territoriality.

When it comes to abilities, love birds usually don't learn how to talk but they can be trained to do tricks which are something that we'll also talk about later in this book. They can be easily housetrained, and litter trained as well. If you truly want to bond with your pet then teaching them all these things, and a trick or two can create a great relationship for both for you.

A lovebird need daily interaction and should always be handled so that they can feel affection from you as their keeper, and makes it also easy on your part to socialize them with other bird species and people.

When it comes to feeding them, certain species will require particular types of bird nutrition. There's a one – type – fits – all though in general it's best that you feed them with commercial diet or pelleted diet combine with fresh fruits and vegetables so that they can achieve a balance diet. You may also need to give them supplements and other vitamins/ minerals depending on their age or condition.

Introduction

Feeding your lovebird the right nutrition is definitely essential to its health and also longevity. Some owners succumb to just giving bird seeds and water to their pets but doing this just won't cut it. Changing their diets constantly is also not advisable though of course you can change it from time to time but in a gradual way. The important thing is that you provide them with a healthy variety and also strike a balance of a delicious treat so that they'll get excited when eating.

When it comes to their health, lovebirds are quite susceptible to various types of illnesses which are oftentimes caused by improper diet. They can become obese and suffer from liver diseases or digestive problems. They can also become infected with bird viruses, poxes, parasitic and bacterial infections as well as bird syndromes. They can also become susceptible to other physical problems like crooked beaks, constricted toes, splay legs, and other physical injuries that are usually caused by improper husbandry and breeding practices or genetic factors. We will discuss all of these and how you can prevent and treat such common illnesses to keep your lovebirds healthy.

They are also perfect companions even if you live in a small apartment because they don't need to live in a big cage unlike other birds. They're also not that loud although sometimes they tend to sing or quack a lot. Nevertheless, it's not to the point where your neighbors will come knocking at

Introduction

your door to complain about the loud noises. They're also easy to maintain and handle but can be a bit of a challenge as well especially for newbie keepers. Later in this book, we will provide you with everything you need to know about keeping these lovebirds as pets and a general guideline when raising birds.

If you're able to provide well for your lovebird in terms of its basic needs and affection, then you and your newfound pet will have a wonderful time together!

Introduction

Chapter One: Basic Biological Information

Lovebirds are named as such because they are one of the few animal species that are monogamous when it comes to finding a mate. They also develop a loving and strong bond with their chosen pair. However, as sweet as it may sound, there are some instances where this is not the case. Some lovebirds don't bond with one bird forever because of incompatibility. Nonetheless, when these birds bond with their mates, it tends to be long – term compared to other animal species. If ever you choose to keep a male and female lovebird, you'll eventually see that they'll snuggle and preen one another, and even provide food for each other.

Chapter One: Basic Biological Information

Lovebirds are also called "pocket parrots" because they resemble the physical characteristics of parrots as well as their intelligence and abilities. Don't be fooled though because that means that these birds are clever, and because of that they tend to be quite bossy with other bird species and family members. Some of them can imitate human voice but unlike parrots, they can't articulate it or most of them never learn to speak.

They form great and strong relationships with their owners making them one of the most popular bird species as pets but it's also important that they find a mate to spend time with aside from their keepers because if not, then you as the owner will need to fill in their strong desire for affection. If you don't spend time with your lovebirds, they'll have a tendency to become aggressive, and it'll be very hard to gain their trust and love which is why if you don't have the time to do that, then it's best to get a pair of these so that they won't be lonely, although starting with one is highly recommended and ideal for newbie keepers.

These birds are cheerful and energetic. They come in different colors, sizes, and types. This chapter will focus on the basic biological information of lovebirds and the things you can expect to learn as we guide you on how to take care of them.

Chapter One: Basic Biological Information

Appearance

Lovebirds look a lot like parrots, but the main difference is that they are small and quite chubby versions of it. It sports a short tail with large hooked upper beaks. Lovebirds usually come in different colors but the most common body color is green especially those that are found in the wild. There are some types of lovebirds that possess a white colored ring around their eyes such as the Fischer's lovebird, black – masked lovebird, yellow – collared, and the black – cheeked lovebird species. There are many colored mutations of lovebirds that have been produced today depending on what kind of combination the breeders would like to produce.

Size

Lovebirds measure between 13 and 19 centimeters or 5 to 7 inches in body length. These birds have an average weight of 40 to 70 grams or around 1.5 to 2 ounces. These lovebirds are one of the smallest parrots in the world. One of the most common types of lovebirds is a species called Peach – faced; it is also one of the largest and heaviest lovebird species because it weighs around 50 to 60 grams.

Chapter One: Basic Biological Information

Distribution / Range

There are 8 lovebird species that originated in Africa, and 1 species that is from Madagascar. The most popular lovebird in the U.S. and perhaps in the world is Peach – faced lovebird because it is charming, and it's also available in various color mutations. The black – masked lovebird and Fischer's lovebird are also common species that are kept as pets.

Diet and Feeding

Once you buy or adopt a lovebird you can change its diet to a pelleted diet especially it's on a seed only type of diet. You can convert their nutrition but make sure to do it gradually so that they can also adjust to it. Generally, birds are creatures of habit, and keeping them are very similar to raising children. If your lovebird had been on a certain type of diet, you can expect it to be quite reluctant at first to eat another type of nutrition since they are not familiar to the taste. Usually, an all seed diet is much more enticing for the birds because it's more delicious since it's rich in carbs and fats unlike pelleted type of diet, therefore it's important to introduce it and do it slowly through feeding it for over a certain period, say around 1 to 2 months or more especially if your lovebird is quite stubborn. Generally speaking, younger birds are much easier to be converted to a new type of diet than older ones.

Chapter One: Basic Biological Information

If you want to get recommendations on how to do this, it's wise to consult your vet particularly during your first visit so that you'll have an idea on what to do or feed your baby bird. Later on in this book, we'll discuss further about what kind of diet you can feed for your lovebirds.

Health and Longevity

It's essential to take your pet bird to a qualified and legit avian vet as soon as possible so that your pet can undergo through physical examination, fecal check – up, and also have its blood sample taken so that you can be sure that your pet has no other underlying illnesses and is generally healthy. If you're having trouble in finding an avian vet you can go to the website of the Association of Avian Veterinarian at <www.aav.org>. A thorough physical checkup after you buy your bird will ensure that you have acquired a healthy pet. Your vet can also provide information about how to keep your bird healthy, make it strong against diseases through recommending the right nutrition, and also the proper vitamins/ supplements that your bird needs to take at certain ages.

Make sure to bring your pet bird to the vet at least once a year, after its initial general checkup so that your pet can have regular wellness exam and other things that your vet will recommend.

Chapter One: Basic Biological Information

Lovebirds has a lifespan of around 10 to 12 years if given a balanced nutrition and diet as well as proper husbandry practices, and of course tender love and care!

Behavior and Temperament

If you like to keep a lovebird species, it's highly recommended that you just keep one (at least for now or, until you can get used to caring for this type of bird) because if you acquire two or more, what will happen is that your pets will bond with one another instead of bonding as much with you. However, your lovebirds will tend to not socialize with people and could also become aggressive towards you or others. You can of course buy at least 2 since they're "lovebirds," but they can still eventually attack or kill one another. If you really wanted to acquire more than 1 bird, it's best that you keep them in separate cages. On the other hand, if you'll stick with one lovebird, the tendency is that it will be more interactive and sociable. Of course, regardless whether you are acquiring one or more birds, the bottom line is that you need to make sure that you provide them with adequate attention, time, and their basic necessities that they deserves. Having only one bird is best for newbie keepers because it will ensure that both of you will have fun and great time together.

Chapter One: Basic Biological Information

When it comes to their nippy behaviors, it is quite natural for them to become aggressive at times especially if they have competitors for their lover's affection! Animals in general tend to become dominant and are naturally territorial. Sometimes, lovebirds and other similar bird species can be housed together provided that the enclosure is large enough to accommodate all of them and avoid territoriality because if that's not the case, they will fearlessly fight for their own space by biting off the toes of other bird species. This is why it's best to make sure that if you're going to acquire more than one, smaller birds must be kept away in separate enclosures.

They may also become aggressive towards other birds that are smaller than them, making them attack one another resulting in bird injuries and sometimes fatality.

It's also not advisable to leave your lovebirds alone with your other household pets like cats or dogs because they can get killed. Make sure to supervise their interactions with other animals or as much as possible avoid introducing larger animals to birds because they will only see them as preys.

Chapter One: Basic Biological Information

Breeding

When it comes to breeding it is best that you kept the birds in a colony system (though this may not be applicable for some other types of species). What breeders usually do in order to achieve great results is to group 5 to 6 pairs of lovebirds, and house them in an aviary or huge enclosure that measures around 10 feet in length by 3 feet wide. Some breeders tend to mate their pets using the so called cabinet system where the birds are placed in a 30 x 20 x 20 inches enclosure or cabinet. We will discuss more about breeding basics later in this book should you be interested in becoming one.

Fun Facts about Lovebirds

Fun Fact #1: Lovebirds feed one another! This is their unique way of forming and maintaining their strong bond with their mate! This can also occur when one of the pair is distress due to a long period of separation. Often times, it will look like they are kissing but in reality, they are giving food to one another.

Chapter One: Basic Biological Information

Fun Fact #2: Lovebirds suffer from "Heartbreak Syndrome" if they are separated from their mate. According to vets, this behavior is somewhat similar to depression that humans feel. In fact, the heartbreak syndrome can cause a lovebird to die if their mate is separated from them for a long time. Sometimes, they can also feel this when their owners are not around often this is because lovebirds have very high levels of "love hormones" or oxytocin in their brains, making the connections they form (with either another bird or human) meaningful. This is also why they earned their name because they really can't stand to be alone, they need to have a pair and form a deep bond. Many lovebirds can also live long and happy lives with a human companion.

Fun Fact #3: There are nine species of lovebirds to choose from. However, only 3 are best kept as pets because the rest are usually wild animals and not domesticated species. They are distributed in Africa and dates back to around 2 million years! They are now found in different continents around the world, thanks to different breeding programs by bird enthusiasts.

Fun Fact #4: Love birds are the 4th popular bird as pets in the U.S. This is because they are not just physically charming but also crazy and smart at the same time! When left to their own devices, they can easily put on a show for themselves, and amuse their mates by doing different tricks. And because they are very active pets, you need to ensure that they have a spacious enclosure, and they should also be provided with mentally stimulating toys to keep bird boredom at bay.

Fun Fact #5: Lovebirds love to go inside hollowed spaces! This is why it's best that you provide huts or nest boxes inside their enclosure because they like to snuggle in these kinds of locations, and they like something cozy.

Fun Fact #6: Out of the nine lovebird species, 7 of them are androgynous. This means that you won't be able to distinguish a male from a female. They also tend to have this mating ritual in the wild, where they will put nesting materials in their feathers to show to their potential mate that they are "husband/wife" material.

Chapter Two: Different Lovebird Species

There are about nine species of lovebirds that are classified under the *Agapornis* genus. Out of the nine lovebird species, eight of them are distributed in many countries in Africa, with one species ranging in Madagascar. Out of the nine species, only 3 of them are popularly kept as pets because the rest are wild birds. These are the Peach – faced lovebird, Black – Masked lovebird, and Fisher's lovebird. These lovebirds are very popular in United States, in Europe and in many countries around the world. They come in wide array of color from peach to teal, and white to green. There are over 100,000 color mutations that exist today – thanks to the enthusiastic lovebird hobbyists.

Chapter Two: Different Lovebird Species

This chapter will cover the popular lovebird species and also give you a brief background of the other lovebirds in the wild.

Peach-faced Lovebird (*Agapornis roseicollis*)

This lovebird species is the most popular pet bird in the United States, and even in many countries around the world. They hail from Southwest Africa, and dates back in the 1700's. Peach – faced lovebirds in the wild are usually seen in flocks of 10 to 30. It has a huge distribution particularly in Phoenix, Arizona because the temperatures and climate there are somewhat similar to their natural habitat in Africa. These birds love to nest around palm trees and cactuses.

Breeders and avian enthusiasts love rearing peach – faced lovebirds because aside from the fact that they are easy to breed, they are also great parents to their offspring. They are available in many vibrant colors today. It has over 100,000 color mutations, making them one of the bird species that comes in multiple colors aside from the budgie parrots. Breeders mix and match pairs so that they can produce their desired color mutation or perhaps create a new one. Avian hobbyists love creating new color mutations because aside from being a rare species, it will also hiked up the cost for their lovebirds.

Chapter Two: Different Lovebird Species

Peach – faced lovebirds are very easy to tame, has a cheerful personality, clever, and is "small but terrible." This is because they tend to become aggressive to other birds and even household pets larger than them. They are perfect for owners living in small apartments because they don't require spacious enclosures, and they're not noisy neighbors. They also love to be in a cozy sort of environment unlike other larger parrot species. They can live up to 20 years if proper nutrition is given.

Peach – Faced Lovebird Specs:

- An average adult is 15 centimeters in length

- The most common color mutations are the following:
    - Lutinos
    - Pieds
    - White – face
    - Orange – face
    - Violets
    - Dutch Blue
    - Mauves
    - Creminos
    - Cinnamons

- This lovebird sports a green plumage, grey – colored feet, blue rump, horn – colored beak, and of course, a peach – colored face hence its name.

- Male and female Peach – faced lovebirds are not sexually dimorphic although some experts can distinguish a male from a female, but it's not always accurate. DNA sexing is highly recommended if you want to know the identity of your lovebird.

Black - Masked Lovebirds (*Agapornis personatus*)

The next most popular household pet lovebird is the black – masked lovebird, also known as the Yellow – Collared lovebird. It may be referred to as Masked Lovebird. Similar to a peach – faced lovebird, they have a chunky and small body. They are originally distributed in the northern and central regions of Tanzania in Africa particularly found in plateaus and brushwood. Some flocks of black – masked lovebirds occur in coastal areas and the eastern region of Kenya.

This lovebird species dates back to the late 1800's, and are only imported to other countries in 1920. Blue – colored mutations of the black – masked lovebird were also discovered in the wild, and were also imported after its

Chapter Two: Different Lovebird Species

introduction. Similar to peach – faced, masked lovebirds like to be in a flock and also tends to form small colonies in their natural habitats. In captivity however, they are not comfortable in a single enclosure as they prefer to be in an aviary setting where they have lots of space.

They became widely popular in the U.S. and even in Europe, and since then many bird breeders took part in producing different color mutations for this lovebird species. They are usually named after their body color such as blue – masked lovebirds, violet – masked, and green – masked but it's understood in the avian community that it is the black – masked species.

Black – Masked Lovebird Specs:

- Black – masked lovebirds measures about 14 ½ centimeters in length or around 6 inches.

- They usually sport a green body color with its head covered in black shade, and its plumage is a yellow collar, although there can be some exceptions.

- Males and females are hard to distinguish. Hens are usually bigger in size with a slightly small and rounded head.

Chapter Two: Different Lovebird Species

- The rump has a shade of greyish blue color, and their abdomen and body area are usually covered in yellow – green.

- Their under – tail coverts are also yellow – green but their under – wings are grey – blue in color.

- Their upper wings have a shade of dark green, while their flight feathers are black in color.

- The forehead of the bird as well as its lores, cheeks, and neck area under its beak is brown – black in color while its back head has a shade of dirty olive.

- The upper chest sometimes has an orange – red colors or yellow color.

- Their tail is green, with an orange – yellow shade on their outer tail feathers.

- They have white rings around their eyes, and their bills are red in color.

- They have grey colored legs and feet.

Chapter Two: Different Lovebird Species

- Sometimes Masked Lovebirds are combined with a Fischer's Lovebird producing a reddish brown shade in the head but it is still called as masked lovebird.

- The most common color mutations are the following:
    - Blue – mutation
    - Yellow – mutation
    - Albino

Fischer's Lovebird (*Agapornis* fischeri)

The next most popular lovebird species is called Fischer's Lovebird. These birds are very beautiful species and are often compared to the witty and playful Peach – face lovebirds. Perhaps the main difference is that Fischer's lovebirds are not as sociable and friendly compared to Peach – faces but there are many breeders who have produced friendly Fisher's lovebird based on their genetic traits since it is a major factor in shaping the personality of a bird. There are many Fisher's lovebird breeders who say that they have a really loving bird, and this is perhaps mostly because of how these breeders socialize their birds from a young age.

As you may now know, lovebirds in general tend to be nippy at times and sometimes they are also scared of people. Skittish and aggressive lovebirds can be trained and

Chapter Two: Different Lovebird Species

taught to be good and friendly pets but of course it will take some time and attention. If your lovebird is not comfortable around you, aggressive or scared when handled that usually means that it hasn't formed a bond with its owner. You have to understand your bird's body language so that you'd know how to approach it and tame it. Once you've done that then it can start warming up on you and become more affectionate.

Just like peach – faced lovebirds and masked lovebirds, Fisher's lovebirds are not loud around the house, and also very easy to maintain. It's a comic – relief bird for the family because of its playful personality. The average lifespan of this species is around 15 to 20 years, but there had been some who lasts for 25 to 30 years!

Fisher's Lovebird Specs:

- Fisher's Lovebird is one of the smaller species among its other kin. It measures about 14 centimeters or around 5.5 inches in length, and has an average weight of 42 to 58 grams.

- Its body color is green which includes its chest, back and also wings. It has a splash of golden yellow color in its neck that progresses to dark orange.

Chapter Two: Different Lovebird Species

- It has an olive – green shade of color on its head, and has a bright – red colored bill.

- The upper plumage has blue or purple feathers.

- It also has a white circle in its eyes similar to peach – faced lovebirds.
- Young Fisher's lovebirds have many similarities to an adult or older bird though the former has is much duller in body color, and their beak's bases have splashes of brown colors.

- The most common color mutations are the following:

    o Pied
    o Lutino
    o Albino
    o Dilute Blue
    o Dilute Yellow
    o Black – Eyed White
    o Dark – Eyed White
    o Cinnamon

Chapter Two: Different Lovebird Species

Rare Lovebird Species Found in the Wild

Abyssinian Lovebirds

Also referred to as Black-winged Lovebirds, this is one of the largest in the Agapornis family. It has a length of around 15 to 17 centimeters or around 6 to 7 inches up to its tail. It has an average weight of 48 grams or 1.5 ounces. Female Abyssinian lovebirds are much heavier compared to males with the former reaching around 53 grams, while the latter only has an average weight of 44 grams.

Compared to the top 3 popular lovebird species, Abyssinian lovebirds are sexually dimorphic and are not visually identical, which means that males and females can be visually distinguished through their physical bodies and qualities. Below are the differences between male and female Abyssinian lovebirds:

Male Abyssinian Features:

- The plumage is usually covered in emerald green color and it also sports a metallic sheen under the sun.

- The green color is relatively lighter on its head, under – tail coverts, and rump.

Chapter Two: Different Lovebird Species

- Males have a bright red – colored forehead that extends into its eye area.

- Its eyes have a narrow ring of red - colored feathers.

- Its cheeks have a splash of yellow – brown colored feathers.

- The flight and wing feathers are covered in green color. Its under – wing coverts are black in color.

- The tails of the males are green in color with a black tip and some yellow marking at its base.

- Its iris color in the eyes has a shade of dark brown

- It possesses a coral red – colored bill and has grey legs and feet.

Female Abyssinian Features:

- The females have a green colored body, with a darker shade of green on its back.

- The females have no red and black markings on its body like in males.

- Similar to males, it has a coral – colored red bill with grey feet and legs.

Juvenile Abyssinian Features

- Juvenile Abyssinian lovebirds look very similar to an adult female Abyssinian, though the under wings in juvenile males are black in color.

- Juvenile females Abyssinian have green colored wing feathers that turn into brownish – black color as they grow old. Their beak's base sports a dusky yellow shade.

Lilian's Lovebird

Lilian's lovebird is one of the smallest lovebird species found in the mainland region of Africa. Its body is somewhat similar to Fisher's Lovebird but relatively larger, and also look a lot like a Peach – faced Lovebird. This species is usually found in many countries in Africa including Zimbabwe, Tanzania (southern region), Zambia (eastern region), Mozambique (North – western side), and Malawi. It is now in Liwonde National Park, and mostly inhabits forests outside the park. Lilian's Lovebird inhabits

Chapter Two: Different Lovebird Species

woodlands, fig trees, and riparian forests. However, this species is being restricted as it is becoming more and more exploited for agricultural purposes.

Lilian's Lovebird Characteristics:

- It has an average length of 5 inches or around 13.5 centimeters, and has an average weight of 28 to 37 grams.

- The plumage of the Lilian's lovebird is covered in green color as well as its tail coverts.

- They also sport red – brown eyes with white colored rings on their eyes.

- The bill is red in color and its throat and forehead area is either orange or red in color.

- Their crown has a shade of salmon – pink as well as its face and upper chest.

- Its lateral feathers are black in color with a tinge of yellow – orange in its tip.

- Both male and female Lilian's lovebird can't be distinguished because they are almost identical.

- Juvenile Lilian's lovebirds have a duller body color with splashes of black on its cheeks, compared to a mature one.

Threats to Lilian's Lovebird

Unfortunately due to natural habitat loss and exploitation, the Lilian's Lovebird is now listed as a Near Threatened species. Although the population is just slightly declining it is still a concern in the avian community. The population of this species was being affected because of floods particularly in Mozambique, and because small – scale farmers consider them as pests. Aside from this, many illegal traders are capturing these birds in the wild and selling them off in black markets especially in Zambia, Mozambique, and Zimbabwe.

It was formerly listed in the Appendix II of CITES around 1981. Today, its population is continuously being monitored because it is still being threatened by predation, natural calamities, and illegal trading/ exploitations.

Black - Cheeked Lovebirds (Agapornis nigrigenis)

The black – cheeked lovebird is the most endangered species with the smallest area of range. They are usually called "eye – rings," and joins the ranks of the Masked, Nyasa and Fisher's Lovebirds since all of them have no feathers in their eyes. These species are previously thought to be under the Nyasa Lovebird or a sub – species of Lilian's lovebird. Today, it is considered a separate species of lovebirds. They had become popular around the 1900s.

Black – cheeked lovebirds are distributed in Zambia (south – west region) particularly in the Kafue River. It was also found in Botswana, and northern region of Zimbabwe but it is believed to be extinct in those areas. They inhabit woodlands, agri areas, and places where fresh water exists. During summer, they come in flocks of up to 500 birds or more. Although they are common in certain areas, they are still vulnerable because of its small and declining population.

Chapter Two: Different Lovebird Species
Black – Cheeked Lovebird Characteristics:

- This species is relatively smaller in size compared to the Fisher's Lovebird.

- It has a green – colored plumage, reddish – brown forehead, and crown with a black face, and brownish – colored throats and cheeks.

- It also has a red bill while juvenile black – cheeks have a more orange – colored beaks.

- Black – cheeked Lovebirds have no confirmed color mutation but it is available as hybrids. You can possibly buy a hybrid of Masked and Black – Cheeked Lovebirds but for a costly price.

Black-collared Lovebirds

The shy type black – collared Lovebirds ranges in the equatorial region of Africa specifically in the forests canopies of the following countries:

- Guinea
- Ghana
- Uganda

Chapter Two: Different Lovebird Species

- Cote d' Ivoire
- Congo Republic
- Cameroon
- Gabon
- Liberia
- Central African Republic

Black - Collared Lovebirds Characteristics

- These shy species of lovebirds is around 5 inches in length or 13 to 13 ½ centimeters up to its tail. It has an average weight of 40 to 41 grams.

- Its plumage is green in color with a slightly paler shade on its back, head, and chest area.

- It is distinguished because of its black half collar marking on its nape area, hence its name.

- Its upper body or the breast area is usually orange in color, or yellowish that progresses into its belly.

- It has a bright blue – colored rump with red markings. Its upper tail feathers are blue while the tip is color red.

- Its beak is color black while its feet and legs are grey. Its irises are yellow in color.

- Males and females are quite identical but the younger black – collared lovebirds have a paler shade of body color with a black band in the back of its neck. The juvenile lovebirds have pale grey – colored beaks, and their irises are brown.

- These lovebird species lives up 10 - 15 years.

Grey - Headed Lovebirds (Agapornis canus canus)

These birds are also called Madagascar Lovebirds. They originated from the island of Madagascar just off the coast of the African continent. Some of these lovebirds are also distributed in other neighboring islands and there were also sightings in South Africa. They usually travel in large flocks in the wild but unfortunately, breeding them in captivity hasn't been generally successful. In the avian community, this means that they are not prolific breeders, and if ever one has successfully bred a captive Grey – headed lovebirds, it will still be tough to introduce because of export restrictions.

Chapter Two: Different Lovebird Species

Grey - Headed Lovebirds Characteristics

- These lovebirds have an average weight of 25 to 36 grams, and it's around 5 to 5 ½ inches in length up to its tail.

- It is the smallest among the lovebird genus, but somewhat in par with the black – collared species although they are much bulky in body structure.

- They have a dark green iris, pale grey – colored bills, feet and legs.

- They are sexually dimorphic because the male grey – headed Lovebirds sports a grey – colored body, while females are green in color.

- Madagascar Lovebirds are very good flyers, and in the wild they can develop high speeds of flight rapidly.

Chapter Two: Different Lovebird Species

Male Grey – Headed Lovebirds Characteristics:

- Has dark green – colored wings and back body

- The chest areas as well as the head are sort of white in color or a light shade of grey

- Its tail has black markings

- Juvenile males have a shade of color green in their heads while their beaks are color yellow.

Female Grey – Headed Lovebirds Characteristics:

- Doesn't have a grey – colored patch on their foreheads

- The body is green in color with a darker shade on its back and wings

- Females have a bright green plumage and a paler shade of green on its chest area.

Chapter Two: Different Lovebird Species

Red - Faced Lovebird (Agapornis pullarius)

Red – Faced Lovebirds have a reputation of being the largest distribution in terms of territory among wild lovebird species. It occurs in equatorial Africa, and is distributed in the following places:

- Sierra Leone, Uganda
- Lake Albert, Uganda
- Northern regions of Angola
- Liberia

These birds are usually found in high forests. In the wild, they live together in flocks of up to 20 – 30 birds after the breeding season. These lovebirds travel long distances to gather food such as crops, different kinds of fruits, and grass seeds. Perhaps the most distinctive characteristics of the Red – Faced Lovebirds are that they are hanging upside down in twigs or branches just like a bat whenever they are roosting or preening. However, captive Red – Faced Lovebirds are also reported to rest upside down which is kind of cool if you think about it. Another fun fact about this lovebird species is that they are one of the first species that were imported in Europe. As a matter of fact, the Duke of Bedford around the 16th century has portraits of this lovely and rare species.

Chapter Two: Different Lovebird Species
Red - Faced Lovebird Characteristics:

- The average length of the Red – Faced Lovebirds is around 6 inches or 15 centimeters with an average weight of 43 grams.

- Its under wing coverts have a lighter shade of green with black feathers that verges into a yellow shade of color in its other under – parts. Generally though, its body is color green.

- Its forehead and faces are usually red in color or sometimes orange – red that extends up to the eyelids, over the forehead as well as the top of its bill and up to its crown.

- The tail feathers and plumage is usually blue in color with a splash of red, black, and yellow rump feathers.
- Their legs and feet are grey in color with brown eyes.

- Females have a somewhat similar body color to males except that it is relatively paler, and females have a red or orange – colored head compared to males.

- The under wing feathers are green in color.
- Juvenile or young Red – Faced Lovebirds have a less extensive orange shaded facial mask compared to

Chapter Two: Different Lovebird Species

matured birds. When it comes to under wing coverts young males sport a black feather while females sport a green feather. Their bills are reddish brown in color with a black mandible.

Chapter Two: Different Lovebird Species

Chapter Three: Acquiring, Feeding and Housing Lovebirds

This chapter will focus on how you can acquire a lovebird from either a rescue center or a lovebird hobbyist. There will be lots of things that we will recommend so that you can be sure that you know where you can best get your pet bird. We will also discuss the initial costs that come when keeping a lovebird or two as well as the things you need to have before you take your pet home. You'll also learn some tips about what to do with your pet on its first few days at your house. This is very important especially for newbie keepers. Finally, you'll learn everything you need to know about providing your pet bird with the right nutrition, and the right housing as well as some maintenance tips.

Chapter Three: Acquiring, Feeding and Housing Lovebirds

Acquiring Lovebirds and Initial Costs in Keeping One

First and foremost before you get a lovebird or any other kinds of parakeet for this matter; you need to make sure you these few things in mind that we're going to talk about.

Get an Avian Vet

The first thing is you want to make sure to get in touch with your local avian vet if you wanted to know the best places or sources to purchase or acquire a pet lovebird. One of the best resources we can recommend in finding a good local vet is by visiting AAV.org (Association of Avian Veterinarian), it's a wonderful resource because you can easily go to their website, type in your details, and voila! You will be given a list of licensed avian vets around your area. It'll surely save you the time and effort in finding a reputable one. Once you do that, you can now choose your avian vet and call them up so that you can be given a list of recommendations of where to acquire a lovebird species that you prefer. You'd most likely be given a list of the parrot or parakeet rescue/ adoption places around your area and perhaps some tips on how to select a healthy lovebird or even a reputable breeder if you want to purchase from a hobbyist.

Chapter Three: Acquiring, Feeding and Housing Lovebirds

Acquire a Lovebird through Adoption/ Rescue

Most avian vets will give you lists of local avian rescue centers; from there you can contact your local avian rescue center and see if you can spend some time with the lovebirds. Usually, rescue centers in the U.S. will do a personality test so that they can match you up with a bird that's quite complementary of your own characteristics. This will help you decide or determine which lovebird or even other bird species is best for you.

Once you've done all that, and have gone through all the steps and the training or other activities that the rescue centers have you do, you can now have the opportunity to foster or adopt through them. When you adopt a lovebird, it's usually at a much lesser cost in your part. The cost of buying a bird from a reputable private breeder versus acquiring one through adoption is very significant. Most times, there's no problem with rescue birds because it's usually rehome or put for adoption because the former owner is deceased or because they no longer can care for it. Aside from the inexpensive cost of adopting a lovebird, the rescue centers also give out different resources that are going to be beneficial for you as a new lovebird owner; this is why it's highly recommended that you first check out your local avian rescue before considering buying from hobbyists because you can literally save lives.

Chapter Three: Acquiring, Feeding and Housing Lovebirds

Many experts will tell you to go with adoption because there had been an ongoing phenomenon where birds and parrots are being exploited, illegally traded, and were suffering from improper husbandry practices just to make a cheap buck.

Acquiring from Breeders and Pet Stores

Some of you may want to purchase a lovebird through other sources like hobbyists or pet stores. If that's the case, then it's best that you get your bird from a reputable breeder instead of buying from pet stores because birds from pet stores are usually bought from breeders that do mass breeding for money's sake, this is where improper husbandry practices usually happen so we advised to as much as possible avoid buying from pet stores. There are a lot of reputable breeders or avian hobbyists that breeds birds out of passion; these are the people you want to acquire your pet bird from. They will help you in becoming a responsible keeper, and you'll also be assured of the quality of the lovebird though sometimes it might be quite expensive compared to just rescuing one. But then again, it's your choice just make sure that the breeder you're going to acquire your lovebird from is legit, responsible, and truly passionate about their birds, and not just because they can make money off of these animals.

Chapter Three: Acquiring, Feeding and Housing Lovebirds

Basic Needs of Lovebirds

Bird Cage

You're going to obviously need a bird cage because this is where you lovebirds will spend most of their time. Usually, birdcages cost around $150 and up depending on the size, quality and the materials or cage accessories included. A standard bird cage usually comes with a perch and stainless steel bowls.

Food Bowls

On top of the bird cage, you'll need to purchase a few stainless steel bowls (around 2 – 3). You don't want to buy a plastic bowl because it holds molds, and bacteria that will be harmful for your pet. Buy stainless bowls instead because aside from it not harboring bacteria, it's also easy to clean in the dishwasher, it's safe, and doesn't hold food smell. You can buy separate food bowls in online stores like Amazon for around $5 and up depending on the size.

Chapter Three: Acquiring, Feeding and Housing Lovebirds

Perches and Toys

Every cage is going to need a certain number of perches, you don't want to overpopulate or over decorate the cage. You can get 2 perches to 3 perches as well as 2 – 3 toys for your lovebird. What you want to do is to keep only no more than 6 things inside the cage. You can rotate toys but make sure not to put them all at once. When it comes to buying perches, you want to make sure that it is sturdy enough. Make sure that you replace the perches after being used for 2 to 3 weeks so that your pet bird's nails don't get filed. The toys should also be mentally stimulating since lovebirds are intelligent creatures and very energetic.

Perches will cost anywhere between $8 to $50 depending on what type you buy

Newspapers

You're going to need lots of newspapers, not for reading though! Many keepers use it to bottom the trays inside the cage. It keeps everything super clean, and very easy to replace – not to mention a recyclable material. Make sure though that whenever you're using it, your lovebird won't walk in it because the ink can seep into their feet and cause health problems. If you don't have newspapers, then paper towels will do.

Chapter Three: Acquiring, Feeding and Housing Lovebirds

Travel Carrier Cage

This will cost you around $89 and up depending on the size and brand, and this is sort of your version of Pandora's Box. A travel carrier cage is important if you love to go road tripping with your family, or if you need to simply get your lovebird to the vet as it will need to be transferred safely. You can line the bottom with paper towels or newspapers as long as you're going to have a short non – extended stay; your lovebird is good to go. You're also going to need a new perch which will cost around $8 to $15. When you see the perch starting to fray, you need to replace it. Don't buy a plastic perch because it'll be slippery for your lovebird, and will most likely cause injuries especially if you're travelling with your pet.

Misting System or Spray

You're going to need regular baths for your bird which is why you need to invest in a misting system or a spray bottle. This is a good way for you to ensure that their skin and feathers stay healthy to avoid becoming dehydrated if ever the environment lacks humidity. You can get a spray bottle for about a dollar or so.

Chapter Three: Acquiring, Feeding and Housing Lovebirds

Cleaning Products

You need to buy wipes, paper towels, soap, cleaning detergent, and wash cloths. Paper towels are a major necessity when keeping any kinds of birds; you'll use it for wiping, cleaning after your bird, and drying stuff up.

Bird Food

Every bird will need seeds as treats. You want to get seeds that will promote an active healthy diet for domesticated birds. You can give your bird with 2 to 4 seed treats a day. Seed treats may cost you around $11 and it will usually last for about 2 to 3 months depending on how many you feed your lovebird.

The next major cost is the natural pelleted food. This is your lovebird's primary diet; you can also add other fruit blend feeds. On top of the regular diet, you'll need to provide your lovebird with a teaspoon of fruit and veggies (preferably high in beta carotene). Such fruits and vegetables include mangoes, kale, cantaloupe, spinach, and broccoli. You can mix it up as well (more about this later).

Chapter Three: Acquiring, Feeding and Housing Lovebirds

First Few Days Home

The first thing to do once your new acquired lovebird arrives in your home is to transfer your bird from the travel cage to his/her actual bird cage. You need to get the bird out of the travel cage, so what you need to do is bring the travel box near the bird cage and balance the box on the edge of the cage door so that it wouldn't slide around and you lose control of it. After doing that, you need to carefully and slowly open the door to the food bowl. This is why it's important in getting the appropriate cage size (which we will discuss in later sections) because it will be much more difficult for you in trying to get your bird out of the box if the cage is too big or too small.

From there you can lure your lovebird with a bowl filled with treats until he/she will eventually reaches his/her actual cage. Once you've successfully done that, you need to close the door and walk away.

Now if you purchase your lovebird from the pet store, you don't just leave your pet in a separate room or at the back of your house because your bird is not use to that since they are used to constant stimulation and interaction from people viewing them in pet stores. Birds from pet stores need to be placed in the center of the living room or a location where there's foot traffic.

Chapter Three: Acquiring, Feeding and Housing Lovebirds

The next thing to do is to earn the trust of your newfound lovebirds. You can start doing that by always offering fresh food and water every single day at least for the whole first week coupled with daily morning greetings, and you calling them by their names. You need to throw the old food from yesterday, and replace it with fresh food using a newly washed stainless bowl or another brand new bowl (which is why you'll need at least 2 to 4). The reason why you need to offer the food in an appropriate bowl is that it will create noise that will make your lovebird excited to eat, and because it's much safer than using plastic ones.

You can then talk to them calmly while feeding them on the side of the cage. What you need to do is to just slide the food bowl inside the cage. Do not open the door, do not stick your hand out inside the cage or hand fed your bird, do not handle your bird in its first few weeks. This is very important, regardless of your bird's age, type or where it was acquire or how it was raised. Do not handle them in the first few days to a week; this is because parakeets and parrots are naturally fearful which is why you need to earn their trust and be patient with them. Once you've built your trust to your lovebird overtime, it will assume that you are part of their flock, and once that happens it'll be much easier to build a relationship with them, handle them, train them, and keep them happy. Make sure to always leave a treat behind every time you go out and say goodbye to them.

Chapter Three: Acquiring, Feeding and Housing Lovebirds

When nighttime comes, it's important to ensure that all the lights are off in the room because it will keep them awake. You can cover half of the bird cage with a towel every night, and just uncover it every morning.

Leave your lovebirds alone for the first 7 days, and follow the tips aforementioned so that your pet will become a confident parakeet inside of its cage.

Identification for Your Lovebirds

When it comes to identifying your lovebirds and keeping them safe, the lovebird you have purchased may or may not come with a leg band. Leg bands functions as your bird's identification card. It usually contains the information about the bird, when the bird has hatched, and other important information from the breeder of your pet like the state where your breeder is doing his business etc. It's up to you if you want to remove your lovebird's leg band as some people don't like to have leg band on their bird's feet while some don't mind. However, it's important if you want your lovebird to be permanently identified. If ever your bird is fidgeting with its leg band, you can have your avian vet remove it for you.

Chapter Three: Acquiring, Feeding and Housing Lovebirds

Aside from the leg band, some owners choose to have a microchip implanted on their lovebirds. Microchipping in birds is pretty much the same procedure that is used in other household pets like dogs and cats. This is the process where vets surgically implant a chip under the animal's skin. The chip contains the owner's information or the bird species information so that they can be identified if ever they get lost. Leg bands and microchipping are the legally recognized form of identification for household pets and other animals in general.

It can be quite important if you are always say, travelling with your pet lovebird or you love to take them outside the house because it lessens the risk of them totally getting lost. If you're not sure whether or not it's good for your bird to be microchipped or not, it's best to consult your avian vet so that he/she can further explain to you the benefits of doing so as well as the process and also how much it would cost for the procedure.

Feeding Your Lovebirds

In this section you'll learn what to feed your lovebirds to ensure that they stay active and healthy. What you can offer them is a mixture of commercialized pellets that doesn't use any artificial coloring. You can also add in oats,

Chapter Three: Acquiring, Feeding and Housing Lovebirds

spelt, whole grains, and mullet. A bad diet is foods that are high in fats, if that's the case then your lovebird can be prone to obesity which can be life – threatening in the long run. If you want your pet to become leaner, healthier, and more active, then the diet that you should provide them should be composed of mostly grains (should make about 20% of their diet), and not just seeds. You can feed them a seed diet but it shouldn't make up more than 10% of the bird's diet. 40% of their diet should be commercial pelleted mix.

Aside from that, you need to offer your pet with fruits and veggies. You can offer slightly thin cuts of cucumbers; you can also use artichokes, baby greens, broccolis, small sprouts, apples, and other tropical fruits. They love greens but you have to introduce it to them gradually. More or less what's safe for people is safe to offer for your lovebirds but there are of course some exceptions such as avocados, chocolates, caffeine, and other toxic matters. Birds are omnivores, you can feed them commercial pellets, grains, nutria fruit blends, fresh fruit slices and veggies, and of course fresh and clean water.

When picking a commercial food, it's important that it contains natural ingredients, and don't use any sort of fillers. If ever you have more than one lovebird, then make sure that you provide multiple feeding and drinking stations so that they won't fight over the food you offer them. When thinking about what to feed your lovebirds, always keep in

Chapter Three: Acquiring, Feeding and Housing Lovebirds

mind how they do it in the wild so that you can understand their psychology better.

For an average size lovebird, you need to feed around 1 to 1 ½ tablespoons of commercial pellets per day. Of course this amount will vary depending on the kind of pellet or food you offer, and the size or age of your lovebird. It's highly recommended that you consult your avian vet so that you'll know exactly how much to feed your bird, how often, and the nutrients he/she will need.

When it comes to your lovebird's appetite, chances are that they won't be able to eat all the pellets or grains that you'll feed them every day, make sure that you throw away all the uneaten foods and always put fresh ones because if you don't, the uneaten foods will harbor bacteria and molds which will be bad for your bird's health as it can become contaminated. So it's best to put a smaller amount and just add a little more if need be to also avoid too much food waste on your part. Whenever your lovebird is eating, it's also important to closely monitor them; this is one way of knowing if your lovebird is not ill because sudden loss of appetite may indicate that your pet is sick. It's best to monitor them to know if your bird isn't eating as it normally would so that you can contact your avian vet as soon as possible.

Chapter Three: Acquiring, Feeding and Housing Lovebirds

Food for Your Lovebirds

#1: RoundBush

This brand mostly sells commercial pellets for parakeets such as lovebirds, and parrots alike. It contains all necessary nutrients that your bird needs. Compare to just offering a seed diet, your bird won't be quite picky because it all looks the same and also tastes the same. You can purchase mini sizes and large sizes of the RoundBush brand. Lovebirds love this food brand in general and it's also what most keepers prefer feeding to their pets.

#2: Lafeber Nutriberries

You can give this to your lovebird before bedtime. You shouldn't feed your birds with seeds before bedtime because they can become overweight. This is a treat that is much healthier for your pet. Many vets also recommend this food brand because it's healthier than regular seeds. It contains seeds, pellets, dried fruits and veggies like bell pepper, mango and other kinds of greens, perfect for when your bird is foraging.

#3: Psittacus Food Brand

Chapter Three: Acquiring, Feeding and Housing Lovebirds

This is quite a new brand, but has been receiving some positive reviews from hobbyists online. Some lovebirds don't like it though maybe because of the hard texture, some birds will prefer foods that are easy to chew on. However, you can use this as an additional food to your recipe.

#4: Seed Pellets

You can still feed your lovebirds with seed pellets from time to time, provided that it's not their only diet or doesn't make up most of their diet as what we've mentioned earlier. There are seeds that are specifically made for lovebirds, so you want to make sure you buy that one although you can mix it with other types of seeds to ensure that your lovebirds get a varied diet.

You can also serve your bird with hemp seeds instead of sunflower seeds since the latter contains high fats.

#5: Treat Box Food Brand

You can buy a ready - made treats for your lovebirds like a treat box. It's usually filled with various treats like walnuts, dried pineapple, and raisins that you can serve to

Chapter Three: Acquiring, Feeding and Housing Lovebirds

your bird as a snack. You can also buy a pumpkin mix that contains dried pumpkin seeds which you can add to their pelleted diet. You can also purchase a quick gourmet which contains some dried veggies such as beans, corn, and peppers but you may need to boil it with hot water. Aside from this, you can also give them other treats like almonds in a shell so that they can crack it. You may also need to add other foods as supplements.

Housing Your Lovebirds

When it comes to housing lovebirds, it's important to note that you should never house 3 or more lovebirds together in one bird cage. Experts don't also recommend, lovebirds with other bird species like parrots, parakeets or even budgies because it's dangerous for these animals to be housed together. Birds in general can harm or injure other bird species regardless if it's their own kin or even if they are properly introduced. If you do, you might end up seeing your birds getting battered due to feather picking, scratching, biting off the feet of each other, eating off the beaks as a result of bird fighting which of course, can result to multiple injuries and even death. Never mix species of birds inside a cage, and never mix varying sizes of bird species inside a cage. Small birds like lovebirds may tend to

Chapter Three: Acquiring, Feeding and Housing Lovebirds

launch themselves to larger parakeets which can result to a grueling fight, not to mention the issue of territoriality inside the enclosure.

If you truly want to keep more than 1 lovebird, then make sure that you only add another one, so that you can have only 2 lovebirds inside a cage which is better since they are communal species, and they do prefer a companion. You might want to get male and female lovebirds if you want to keep more than one pet. However, as we've previously mentioned, if you do get a companion for your existing lovebird, you'll end up having a pet that loves each other, and they won't be as bonded to you compare to if you just keep one.

Setting Up a Bird Cage

When it comes to buying a bird cage for your lovebird, it's best that you get something that measures a minimum of 2 foot x 2 foot cage (or 2 square feet of space in every direction). Lovebirds are active birds, and some of them love to have a space where they can flap their wings. It's not wise to get a very tall cage or a round bird cage because if you do, then your lovebird will only utilize the highest horizontal space of the cage which is limiting them if you bought a tall but narrow cage or a round one. It's highly

Chapter Three: Acquiring, Feeding and Housing Lovebirds

recommended that you buy longer cages with the minimum measure aforementioned so that they can use the entire length of the cage to go back and forth, and maximize the space of the enclosure.

Generally, birds don't prefer round cages because it doesn't give them that sense of protection. A lot of times birds, particularly lovebirds like to spend their time in a corner where they'll feel safe, or as we've mentioned in previous chapters, they like to hide inside of huts or boxes because it offers a sense of privacy and safety for them which round cages don't offer but horizontal cages do as they can sit out on a corner. What you can do is to cover part of the cage so that it will act as their safe zone where they can hide.

Bird cages for lovebirds usually cost around $35 from online stores, and around $50 and up from your local pet stores, that of course will depend on the durability of the cage or the quality as well as the different accessories that comes with it. Generally though, the rule of thumb is the bigger, the better.

When it comes to food and water bowls, you want to make sure that it's made out of stainless steel bowls because it's easier to clean, easy to slip inside your bird's cage, and most importantly, it doesn't harbor molds and bacteria or

Chapter Three: Acquiring, Feeding and Housing Lovebirds

leave any food smells unlike plastic bowls. Make sure to clean these bowls everyday with lukewarm to hot soapy water. If you have more than 2 ceramic or stainless bowls, the better because you can just throw it to the dishwasher and have a new replacement. Some bird cages already comes with a bowl feeder that's attached to the little doors so just make sure to thoroughly wash it.

Lovebirds are clever, and quite mischievous at times, so don't be surprised if your pet bird tries to get out and lift up their door cages, just make sure that you use clips that could secure the doors to prevent your bird from escaping.

When it comes to the bar spacing of the cage, you want to make sure that it is close together or at least have a ½ inch bar spacing so that your bird wouldn't be able to squeeze itself into the bars and sneak out. Larger cages may have spaces that are quite big enough for the bird to get out so ensure that when picking out a cage, it has bars that are appropriately spaced for the size of your pet lovebird. You also want to make sure that you buy a stainless type of bird cage because ordinary bird cages are usually painted and your birds can chip away the painting and ingest them which can be toxic for your pet.

If you buy bird cages from pet stores, you might encounter a bird protector. It's supposed to protect your pet

Chapter Three: Acquiring, Feeding and Housing Lovebirds

from mites but they can be dangerous, unnecessary, and ineffective to your bird's health so better get rid of it.

Cage Accessories

There are a lot of things that are important to have for your pet lovebird to experience a happy environment. One of these things is a water bottle; this is in addition to your water bowl since lovebirds usually defecate on their water bowls or whatnot so providing them with water bowls on the side of their cage is ideal because it will enable them to constantly have access to fresh source of water. It also comes in handy whenever you're going to a trip, and you're bringing your pet along. However, you need to make sure that before you take away the water bowl, you need to see them learning how to drink from it or perhaps train them to drink from the water bottle otherwise they might get dehydrated.

The next important cage accessory is a perch with varying diameters or lengths. Never use a plastic perch as it tends to be slippery and can make your lovebirds lose their footing and injure themselves inside the cage. What you want to buy is a stick that has different diameters all along its length or a more natural wood type of diameter. This is because when your lovebirds hold on to their perches, what

Chapter Three: Acquiring, Feeding and Housing Lovebirds

usually happens is that if there's no varying diameter, they'll get sores on their feet because it's in the exact same pressure point every time, and they could also develop arthritis from not being able to have changing diameters since it will cause their leg muscles to get weak. If you have varying diameters of perches, it will wear down your lovebird's nails naturally. If the perch is too wide or too thin, then your bird's nails don't really touch their nails and it'll overgrow which can be hard to clip later on. As long as you have natural perches with varying diameters, then there's no need for you to trim their nails.

You have to also ensure that the highest perch inside the cage is not a wooden dowel; it should be the varying diameter perch. Wooden dowels are ideal as a low perch because your bird will only need to use it occasionally since they don't like being at the bottom of the cage.

You need to also buy 2 to 3 indestructible and mentally stimulating toys which you can easily purchase online or at your local pet store. Lovebirds like to chew up stuff. Females are naturally fond of building nests because that's how they are in the wild so it's also best if you provide them with newspapers that they can shred up and build nests from.

You can also buy puzzle toys where they'll need to figure out how they can get their treats inside. Another type

Chapter Three: Acquiring, Feeding and Housing Lovebirds

of toy that's popular is a skewer. It's a stainless steel rod where you can put small pieces of treats like apples, cucumbers, veggies etc., and you can just hang it up on the bars of the cage. You can also rotate the toys every now and then, and avoid putting too much stuff inside the cage. Ideally, 2 to 3 toys are enough to keep bird boredom at bay.

It's also best that you put up multiple feeding stations for your pets so that they can have more than one option of where to get their food, and they can replicate their natural foraging instincts like what they do in the wild.

Last but not the least is that you want to make sure that everything you'll use inside your bird's cage or the materials you'll buy for their basic needs are non – toxic to avoid any health issues.

Cleaning the Bird Cage Tips

- Make sure to always clean the bottom area of the cage every single day. This is because your lovebirds will constantly defecate, mess up their food, and have splashes of water everywhere which can be a breeding ground for bacteria and molds. If you don't replace it every day, your lovebird will most likely get ill.

Chapter Three: Acquiring, Feeding and Housing Lovebirds

- You need to also provide a cage bedding which can be made out of newspapers, recycled papers, or paper towels that you can buy from supermarkets or pet stores. You need to also put a grate in the bottom so that your bird wouldn't be able to access the bottom of the cage since that's where all the dirty stuff ends up, and you don't want your bird to eat left over or contaminated foods and their fecal matter.

- It's ideal to clean your bird's cage at least once a week. It's best to use hot soapy water, or dilute bleach solution. You can use one part bleach to 30 parts of water.
- After spot cleaning your bird's cage, make sure to rinse it thoroughly and don't left any soapy substance behind and dried it out properly including all the cage accessories before bringing your bird back inside it.

Chapter Four: Grooming and Keeping Your Lovebirds Happy

There are several things you need to keep in mind when grooming your lovebirds; first is you need to give them a bath once in a while; second, is you need to clip or trim their wings or flight feathers; third, is you need to maintain their beaks; and lastly, you need to get their nails clipped. This chapter will provide you with information that will help you in keeping your lovebird/s fully groomed, and always ready to go. Maintaining good hygiene is important so that they will keep their physique, and also make them feel good.

Chapter Four: Grooming & Keeping Your Lovebirds Happy

Grooming Your Lovebirds

The first thing that comes to mind when you talk about grooming is bathing your pet. When it comes to giving your lovebird a bath, it's important to note that birds don't need to take baths as much as other household's pets do such as your cat or dog. What you can do to sort of clean them up is to get a spray bottle filled with clean water, and just spray your lovebird at least once every day. It's just like spraying your orchids or other house plants! This way your bird will naturally preen.

Preening is a bird's way of keeping themselves clean. They usually get rid of dirt or other things in their feathers, keep them neat, and it's their own way of maintaining their feathers in good shape. You might see your pet lovebird do this every day for at least 10 to 15 minutes, and that's completely normal. However, if you see that your pet is plucking his feathers out or doing damage to its own skin that may be considered an abnormal behavior or what is called feather – picking. Usually, there's an underlying illness or symptom of why your bird is doing this kind of behavior, if you always notice this then it's best to ask your avian vet about it.

Another option for bathing your pet or keeping them misted is to take them with you when you shower, and have

Chapter Four: Grooming & Keeping Your Lovebirds Happy

them sit on a little perch or on your towel rod. The splashes of water from your shower may encourage them to preen, and you can supervise them at the same time. Preening is important to keep your lovebird's beautiful feathers in good shape.

How to Bathe Your Lovebirds

When it comes to bathing your lovebirds, don't be surprised if your pet will at first resist it as some actually get startled if you spray them with water or if you attempt other bathing techniques on them. You have to understand that birds are creatures of habit, so if you want to bathe them or mist them every day, they have to get used to it, and it has to be a part of their "routine." It's wise to introduce bathing to them gradually or slowly. Don't spray it directly on their face or eyes, and don't also spray them too much that it will feel as if you're flooding them. Do it slowly, and in little amounts at first.

What you can do if your lovebird gets startled the first time you spray water on them is to just leave the bottle of spray by your bird's cage, and then spray it away from them once or twice a day. That way, your pet will get used to the spray going around and misting the cage as well as the sound and sensation of it. You can do that for a few days

Chapter Four: Grooming & Keeping Your Lovebirds Happy

to a week. Make sure that you spray it on the cage or on your pet's direction, and not directly on them during this introduction period. This way they'll get used to it, and won't get scared of it; they might actually enjoy it after a few days or so. It'll then be part of their habit.

If you choose to take your pet with you while you shower, what you can do is perhaps put them inside their little travel cage, and place it in a location where they'll get a little bit misted. Just like what you did in the spray, you can do that for a few days, and take their cage closer to the shower until they get used to it. Once they do, you can probably let them out of the cage and put them in your towel bar or shower perch so that they can fully enjoy bathing and preening with you! These are good ways of also forming a strong bond with your bird.

Trimming Your Bird's Wings

It's highly recommended to have your bird's wings trimmed because there's a lot that these creatures can get into especially if they are fully flighted. If you've already taught them how to fly or just let them roam around your house, there's a big chance that they can escape, and as far as lovebirds are concern, they are hard to find since they are small types of birds. Aside from that, if you don't trim their

Chapter Four: Grooming & Keeping Your Lovebirds Happy

wings, and they are fully flighted, they can also end up flying into an aquarium, boiling water, oil, or water with detergent, ceiling fans and other things like that wherein they can get injured or killed.

You can trim your lovebird's wings by yourself, and get your avian vet give you a demo on how to do that or you can just bring them to your vet and let them do it for you. It's important to note that if ever you do trim them at home, or bring them to a pet grooming place, only the outer 8 to 10 feathers should be trimmed and not the entire wing. If you cut all their flight feathers, your lovebird will be completely incapable of doing a soft landing should they jump off of their cage or a high counter in your house.

The outer 8 to 10 feathers are primarily used for take - off, and that's what you need to trim so that they won't be able to get fully flighted as these feathers get birds into a higher height. You don't want your pet to end up somewhere dangerous. The inner feathers or the secondary feathers are used for gliding and landing so make sure you don't cut that off.

We highly recommend that you let your avian vet do the wing trimming because that way your bird will also recognize that you're not the one doing the traumatic stuff. This way your lovebird will not associate you with having a negative experience. However, if you do want to cut it yourself, then make sure that you avoid the "blood feathers." These are feathers that aren't fully matured yet, and they can be distinguished by having a darkish shade of shaft. Don't cut these blood feathers because it still have a blood supply, and will definitely result to your pet getting injured and bleeding profusely. If ever you accidentally cut the blood feathers, or your bird did that to himself as a result of jumping inside the cage, then you should take him/her to the vet as soon as possible. It's also best to ask your vet to show you where the blood feathers are located in your bird so that you'll be familiar with them, and also what you need to do as first aid if ever you accidentally cut your pet's blood feathers.

Clipping Your Bird's Nails

When it comes to clipping your bird's nails, most avian vets will advise you to trim it at least every other month or several times a year depending on its growth rate. If the bird is walking on you and it's beginning to do damage in your skin or is uncomfortable then that means it's time to get your bird's nails done. The first nail trim should be done by the vet so that they can properly show you how to do it, if ever you choose to trim it yourself at home. Some avian vets use a grinding stone to dribble the nails down

Chapter Four: Grooming & Keeping Your Lovebirds Happy

naturally, and not trim them. It does help it clipping the nails and making it smoother. At the same time, the grinding stone will stop to serve the bleeding if ever the quick is hit. The quick in birds is the part of the nail that has blood on it.

If ever you do it at home and you accidentally cut off the quick, it might seem like there's a lot of blood, but don't panic because your bird will not die out of that. What you need to do is to just get a styptic powder or a cornstarch/flour and hold it on the bleeding nail because it will help stop the bleeding.

Caring for Your Lovebirds' Beak

When it comes to beak care of your lovebirds, you don't need to actually worry about it because they're pretty good at maintaining their own beaks. What they usually do is that they rub their beaks in their cage's surface or or on itself which helps in maintaining its form or shape. Chewing things like toys can also help in beak maintenance.

You can trim your bird's beak if he/she has a malocclusion. This is a condition where a bird's beak is misaligned making them not properly and naturally worn down causing it to overgrow. If your pet bird has malocclusion, you'll see that their top beak and bottom beak

Chapter Four: Grooming & Keeping Your Lovebirds Happy

is going in different directions, and then overgrowing. If your bird happens to have this then it's best to take them to the avian vet as soon as possible.

The only time you'll need to trim your bird's beak is if he/she are always biting someone. It can help you out while you're working on their biting behavior. If ever your lovebird is aggressively and severely biting anyone, trimming their beaks will only lessen the problem but not necessarily eradicate it. Consult your vet about this so that he/she can guide you on how to fix this aggressive behavior. Trimming your bird's beak is only done for a period of time for aggressive birds while you or your vet is training your pet into not biting anyone.

Chapter Five: Handling, Taming, and Training Your Lovebirds

This chapter will teach you the step by step process of handling your pet in its first few days, then to taming it, and eventually progressing to do basic tricks. This is very important because it will build trust and confidence to your bird, and it will also create a strong bond with you at the same time. When it comes to gaining your pet's trust, the most important thing is patience, and repetition. Never rush things, and be patient as a trainer to do the same things over and over again so that your pet can easily make it part of their habits and routine.

Chapter Five: Handling, Taming & Training Your Lovebirds

Steps in Handling, Taming and Training Your Lovebirds

Below are the following steps and tips you need to do once you've acquired your newfound lovebird. Make sure to follow these steps so that you'll gain the trust of your lovebird in no time!

Step #1: Have a "bird training area"

The first thing you need to do before taming or training your pet is to find a location in your house which will serve as your lovebird's training area. When deciding which place, always keep in mind that the location is parrot – proof which means that the place is safe for your pet bird. You don't want to train them in areas where they are near hazardous objects or your other household pets that can potentially injure your lovebird. Make sure that the room is also secured so as to prevent your bird from escaping or flying away once you let them out of the cage. Keep in mind that lovebirds are small creatures with powerful flight skills. They can easily fly from the cage to the top of the curtains or go under the bed; if you're a newbie keeper, it'll be hard for you to get them back, and even if you do, it'll be traumatizing for your bird.

Chapter Five: Handling, Taming & Training Your Lovebirds

Step #2: Let your lovebird adjust to its new environment

This is something that we've mentioned in previous chapters wherein you'll need to make sure that you provide your bird with fresh food and water as soon as you have transferred him/her in their permanent cage on their first few days. Once you do that, the most important tip is to LEAVE YOUR BIRD ALONE. Allow it to adjust to its new cage, to its new environment, or to the bird training area. Don't handle it for the next few days or so, just provide food and water on its cage, without touching it, and let it relax. Most lovebirds and parakeets in general will need some time to adjust to its new surroundings. You'll most likely notice that it will spend some time at the bottom of its cage – and that's okay. Don't panic, it's just quite anxious about its new home which is why it's important to give them some space. It'll probably take around 3 days to a week or so depending on your lovebird's personality. Some birds tend to adjust quickly, and are social while some are quite skittish, so monitor them and avoid handling it until you see your bird gets used to you and its new place.

Step #3: Start interacting with your pet lovebird

You should do this while simultaneously doing the second step. You can interact with your bird (non – physical interaction) by sitting in front of their cage and simply

Chapter Five: Handling, Taming & Training Your Lovebirds

communicate with them. Don't attempt to touch or handle your bird aside from just sliding up their food/ water bowls. Just talk to your bird, and get it used to your voice, tone, and your actions. If ever more than one person wants to train your pet or interact with it, then it's best that both of you sit down together and communicate with the bird. However, make sure that you don't also crowd up the bird because you'll most probably scare it off. Too much noise and people will overwhelm them and might make them stress on their first few days. Just speak to it in a calm and soothing manner so that they'll eventually recognize you and feel comfortable around you. Do this for about a week or 7 days; 1 week of your bird getting used to the environment, and another for conversing with it. This way they'll get use to you with their new environment which will make you a subset of their new comfort zone.

Step #4: Start placing your hand on the side of the bird's cage (outside)

What you do is to just come into the room or wherever your bird is located, then sit down in front of it and slowly place your hand on one side of the cage. You can do this every day for about 3 days; at least 1 hour during the day, and 1 hour at night. This is to create a good impression to your bird because this is what will eventually build trust.

Chapter Five: Handling, Taming & Training Your Lovebirds

After doing that for 3 days, you can then place your hand on the other side of the cage for another 3 days, then on the top and then on the bottom. Eventually, you'll start seeing that your bird is beginning to adapt to your hand, and recognize it as a moving object that can be seen outside the bird cage. What you need to achieve at this stage is to see your lovebird drink or eat their food while your hand is placed on the cage. This is a sign that your lovebird is already comfortable with you around, and you're ready to move on to the next step.

Step #5: Start placing your hand inside the bird's cage

Once you've noticed that your lovebird doesn't mind your hand being placed outside of its cage, you can now open the door of your bird cage, and then do the exact same thing as you did in the fourth step only this time; you place your hand inside. Put your hand on the left side of the cage for 3 days, on the right side for another 3 days, then on the top and bottom for the next few days. What we're trying to do here is to make your hand a subset of the comfort zone. This stage becomes quite tricky for some people because they usually rush this process. Some newbie keepers, once they get their hand inside, they are always tempted to touch their bird. You should never touch your bird at this stage because it will still be scary for them if you do. You have to

Chapter Five: Handling, Taming & Training Your Lovebirds

follow this tip because this is the foundation of trust for your bird which will be beneficial once you start taming, and training them later on. This introduction process is tedious but it has long – term rewards.

Step #6: Hand feed your lovebird

Once you're done with that, the next step is to hand feed your bird. This step is crucial because you want to make a good impression to your bird, and as what they say "first impressions lasts. " When you hand feed your bird for the first time, you want to make sure that you're calm, slow, and also quite entertaining through communicating with them or interacting with them while you're hand is around the cage. Focus on both verbal and physical interaction. What you need to do is to remove the food bowls for about 1 ½ hours before bird training during the day and at night. Then place the food on your palm, and have the seeds on your hand while slowly placing your hand inside its cage. Don't offer the food to your bird or get your palm anywhere near them. Just place it inside the cage with about 30 cm distance, and let the parakeet naturally come to you. You can do this for about 3 days at least 30 minutes each morning and night. Don't move your palm too much because your bird will get scared, so just keep it steady until your pet comes and eats from your hand. Once they do that, you can gradually get a

Chapter Five: Handling, Taming & Training Your Lovebirds

bit closer to your bird; say 10 cm or so to each passing day. Your bird will eventually get used to your hand feeding, and once that happens, you can now add a unique command each time you hand feed them. This will alert your birds that you will open the cage, and will hand feed them. Some birds tend to forget the whole thing which is why it's important to repeat the process every day and be very consistent with what you do so that they'll remember it and treat it as part of their routine. This is why having a set time to feed or train your bird, doing the same gestures, and saying the same commands is recommended throughout your pet's lifetime because they'll easily learn from it since they are creatures of habit.

Step #7: Ask your lovebird to "step – up"

Now here comes the training part. Stepping – up is one of the basics of bird training. What you need to do is to approach your pet with your hand with the food. You'll then need to carefully get the side of your palm near its chest while saying a command like "up, up" or "come" in an exciting tone to get your pet to step – up. Once it does, do not move, be still, and just let your bird eat the treats in your palm. This is a positive reinforcement to get your pet to step up in your hand, and build trust. Repeat this process for at least 7 days. Still do the basics like placing your hand inside

Chapter Five: Handling, Taming & Training Your Lovebirds

the cage, conversing with it, hand feeding it without imposing to touch it, and commanding it to step – up. Do not change anything, follow your routine, say the same commands, do the same gestures, and just add this one routine. Once your bird becomes fully comfortable with you within these training sessions, and perhaps has mastered the step – up technique. The next thing to do is to ask it to step – up, and add your other palm or hand. You only place food on one of your palms, and you just need to ask it to sort of ladder up or hop on to your other hand, and then continuously ask it to keep stepping – up. You need to do all of these inside the cage not outside. Keep doing it for about 5 days, and let them eat the treats on your hand as it is positive reinforcement. Always be calm and still.

Step #8: Step - up and reward

Once your pet bird has mastered this laddered technique of stepping – up, the next thing is pretty much the same, only this time you'll put treats on your other hand or palm. When you see your bird already fully comfortable with that, then it's time to take it out of its cage.

Chapter Five: Handling, Taming & Training Your Lovebirds

Step #9: Bring your bird out of the cage

For this step, all you need to do is to ask your pet to step up on your finger, and then bring it out of the cage for about a few seconds, and do the ladder technique where you make them step – up from one hand to another, then bring it back inside the cage again. The interval of bringing your pet out of the cage and back inside should be short at first to lessen the risk of your pet flying away. You can gradually increase the interval once your bird becomes confident, and has mastered this step. Repeat the process and always use the commands. Your goal is to make your bird confident in stepping up, and being outside. You'll notice that your bird will wait for you to put your hand back inside the cage before stepping out onto its perch, and not sort of flying. If your pet has successfully done this, make sure to reward them with treats!

Step #10: Use the bird training stand

Before you follow this next step, make sure that you bought a bird training stand because you'll need it for this next routine. Once you have that, what you can do is to bring it out of the cage, and while your pet is eating treats from your palm, you can slowly walk towards where the bird training stand is. Once you've reached the stand, ask your bird to step up in the stand. Do not remove your hand

Chapter Five: Handling, Taming & Training Your Lovebirds

or the treats yet otherwise your pet will associate that being in the stand means no food. Make sure to provide food bowls near the stand if you want your pet to stay a bit longer. Do this back and forth for the next 4 to 5 days until your bird gets habituated with it. If ever your pet flies away, don't panic. Just go where it went and calmly ask it to step up on your hand (filled with treats) so you can bring it back to safety. This is why removing food at least an hour before training is good because it'll get your pet excited for food and rewards.

Step #11: Leave your bird in the bird training stand

This time the routine you'll add is to leave your pet for a few minutes in the bird training stand. You're not going to bring it back and forth to the cage this time, you're going to practice it to stay and be comfortable in the stand. Make sure to keep food and water bowls near it, and put away the cage outside the training area where your bird can't see it. Leave your bird for a few minutes but still under your supervision. When you start to see your bird panic or fidgeting, ask your bird to step up, and bring it back inside its cage. Do the same thing the next few days, and increase the time it stays on the stand away from the cage until your bird can stay for about an hour or so every day, and at night.

Chapter Five: Handling, Taming & Training Your Lovebirds

This will condition your bird to be comfortable in the training stand.

Step #12: Teach other tricks to your lovebird

Once your lovebird has already gotten used to these kinds of routines, you can now start teaching it other tricks. You can continue using the step – up technique or ladder technique using your finger, and rewarding it with treats using your palm. You can then start asking them to step – up on your shoulders from your hand, and then offer a reward. Repeat the trick over and over every time you do training twice a day until it's locked in their memory. Don't rush and be patient. Once you've done all the basics of stepping – up, you can now teach other tricks like flight recall or target technique and other things.

Chapter Five: Handling, Taming & Training Your Lovebirds

Chapter Six: Keeping Your Lovebird Healthy

Lovebirds and birds in general are susceptible to illnesses. Such illnesses are oftentimes caused by various factors such as improper husbandry practices, viral and bacterial diseases, organ infections, breeding problems, and even stress. This is why it's important to have your pet bird checked thoroughly by the vet at least every other month to ensure that he/she is well and in top condition. This chapter will focus on the top 3 most common illnesses of lovebirds; it's causes, symptoms, and treatments.

Chapter Six: Keeping Your Lovebird Healthy

Common Illnesses of Birds

Egg Binding

This happens when a mother bird isn't able to pass an egg out of its system, and the egg gets stuck inside of it. This problem is unnoticeable especially if you don't know which one is male or female. Some owners don't know the sex of their pets, so to speak.

The usual symptoms of egg bonding in females include straining, its feathers are fluffed – up, rapid breathing (since they have an egg stuck in their reproductive system, it can push up on their airways), doesn't like droppings. Female birds that have this problem will show signs of becoming very sick very quickly. Go to your avian vet as soon as possible to have your bird checked out especially if you have males inside the cage or if you just recently bred your lovebird.

Respiratory Infection

This is another common illness that keepers face when taking care of lovebirds and birds in general. If you notice your pet having nasal discharge, or they're sneezing

Chapter Six: Keeping Your Lovebird Healthy

and coughing often then that's a sign that your pet may be suffering from a lung infection. Lethargy can also be seen in birds suffering from upper respiratory infections. This illness can be caused by different kinds of factors such as pathogens (viral, fungal or bacterial), and improper husbandry practices. You may also notice a change in your pet's voice or squeak if your lovebird has a hypothyroid. Their thyroid organ is located in their chest which can swell and might cause that change of voice in your bird or even cause them to vomit.

Heavy Metal Toxicity

This is a very common problem for owners especially newbies because their birds often times get exposed to toxic objects. The bird either ingests it or become constantly expose to various heavy metals that are toxic to them. This is usually caused by the caging materials you used when housing your pet or oftentimes it's because of the various objects found in the household. You'd be surprise that many materials in your house contributes to this toxic that your bird might get exposed to so make sure that before you bring your parrot home or let them roam around your house, the space should be parrot – proof, and remove any toxic chemicals or things that may harm your lovebird's

Chapter Six: Keeping Your Lovebird Healthy

overall health. If your pet is showing signs of lethargy, respiratory infections, or other unusual behaviors, consult your avian vet as soon as possible.

How to Tell If Your Lovebird is Sick

The major sign that your lovebird is sick is when you notice it becoming lethargic or isn't as active as it usual is. What lovebirds usually do if they're not feeling well is to sit in one corner of the cage, and puff their feathers up to make themselves look bigger; they do this to increase their body warmth. The most common cause of illness for lovebirds is cold temperatures since these bird species are naturally tropical birds. These birds need to be kept at a relatively humid temperature around 70 degrees. Cold temperatures can cause them to get ill and experience respiratory infections.

Always inspect your bird and be wary of its physical condition and behaviors. Discharges from the nose, eyes, and also its fecal discharge are indicators if your bird is sick or not. You also want to make sure that there's no bleeding or injuries in its body. Lethargy is the number one indicator as well as seeing your lovebird puff itself up. If you see these behavioral changes often, then it's time to take your pet to

Chapter Six: Keeping Your Lovebird Healthy

the vet because it could signal a disease which can threaten not just the health of your bird but also its longevity.

Treating Lovebirds

You have to understand that birds are flock animals. This means that they will try to as much as possible conceal whatever illness they have or feeling because in the wild, sick or injured birds are oftentimes the target of predators. This is why as a keeper, it's your responsibility to always check – up on them, notice their behaviors, and bring them to a vet at least every now and then to ensure that they don't have any problems because usually owners don't notice the subtle changes in their bird's health or behavior which can be bad because these are the indicators of ill health. Oftentimes the owner will notice changes in the bird's body when it's already too late and the disease have already become worse.

Common signs of an ill pet, aside from the ones we've previously mentioned, include rapid loss weight, loss of appetite (stops eating or drinking which can cause dehydration), unclear distinction of urates (yellow urates), and undefined fecal matter (liquid feces). Feather plucking in birds is also a major sign that there's an underlying illness.

Chapter Six: Keeping Your Lovebird Healthy

When it comes to treating your lovebird, it's important to note that you take him/her to an avian specialist or an avian veterinarian, and not just a general vet. If your dog or cat vet isn't an avian specialist, then ask him/her to recommend you to someone who is.

Paying attention to your bird and following your vet's advised are keys in ensuring that your bird is happy and healthy.

Chapter Seven: Basic Breeding Tips

Rearing baby lovebirds is a difficult endeavor to undertake for experts especially for newbie keepers such as yourself. This is why it's best to ask yourself the reason why you want to breed these creatures. You'll need to make sure that you have the time, patience, financial capacity, and the space to breed and raise lovebirds or any other species for this matter. It will be very difficult for you if this is your first time keeping a pet so we highly discourage it. You don't want to end up with a lot of dead baby birds due to improper husbandry practices or lack of time and attention. Nevertheless, if you plan on becoming a breeder in the future, this chapter will give you an overview of what to expect.

Chapter Seven: Basic Breeding Tips

Breeding Your Lovebirds

The actual breeding of lovebirds isn't difficult. It's raising and rearing baby lovebirds is time consuming. Basically, you just get a healthy male and female lovebirds which can be of different lovebird species, get them in the cage, and give them time and space so that they can naturally mate with one another.

Tip #1: Healthy parents make healthy babies

If you decide you're going to breed your pet with another bird/s, then make sure that both of them are in top condition. What you can do beforehand is to visit your avian vet, and make sure that they're both healthy and capable of breeding especially the female lovebirds. A full check – up will do; of course, it's wise to ask your vet about health and breeding tips so that you can gain insight on the things you should do and keep in mind when breeding these animals.

Tip #2: Prepare an adequate nest

You need to provide a large enough nest that can fit two lovebirds. You can easily buy various types and sizes of nest boxes from your local pet stores or online. This is the place where your birds will mate, and where the mother will want to stay in once she is already fertilized.

Chapter Seven: Basic Breeding Tips

Tip #3: Know the basic of rearing and raising chicks

Lovebirds on average lay 2 clutches every two days until they reach around 6 eggs. It will take around 18 days to hatch. Once these young lovebirds have hatched, you need to take them away from their mother, and start hand – rearing them yourself. This means that you need to care for them most of the day because you need to feed them at least every 5 minutes. This is why rearing and raising chicks is very difficult especially for newbie breeders. Baby birds leave their nest after about a month. Make sure that there are no signs of egg binding in your female pet.

The idea of rearing or raising the chicks yourself is to ensure that the bird gets used to being handled by you because it'll be easier to socialize it in the future as well as handle and train it. Make sure that you have a lot of time in your hands before deciding to breed your own lovebirds

Materials for Breeding

- Cuttlebone
- Nesting box
- Quiet space or separate aviary/ cage (with temperatures of around 65 to 75 degrees Fahrenheit)
- Breeding foods or food with extra source of calcium
- Water, fruits, veggies

Chapter Seven: Basic Breeding Tips

Things to do:

- Set up lots of food for the parents at the bottom of the cage or the nesting box to encourage mating or breeding.
- Ideally the bird cage should be 26" long x 14" wide x 20" high.
- When it comes to the nesting box, there should be a concave area for the eggs as well as bedding. Ideally, the size of it is 20 x 12 x 12 cm.
- Provide enough fruits, veggies, and calcium (from cuttlebone).
- Clean the nesting box at least once a week. Make sure that it's dry because wet/damp nests can cause respiratory infections
- Check the nest only once a day.
- Once the chicks have hatched, make sure to feed them always, attend to their needs, and never make any sudden changes in temperature as it could be fatal for them.

Glossary of Important Terms

Addled eggs - These eggs are not viable and will not hatch.

Afterfeather - A structure that projects from the shaft of the feather at the rim of the superior umbilicus.

Allopreening - An act of social grooming amongst birds, in which one bird preens the other or a pair of birds does so mutually.

alternate plumage - The plumage of birds displayed in time for courtship or a breeding season.

Altricial - hatchlings with their eyes closed, and are not capable of leaving the nest on its own, and relies on parents for food.

Alula - a bird's "thumb"

Anisodactylus - a bird foot which has three toes pointing forward and one toe pointing at the back

Anting - a behaviour when birds rub insects, typically ants, on their feathers and skin

Aviculture - captive breeding and raising of birds

Back - exterior area of a bird's upper parts between its mantle and rump

basic plumage - non-breeding plumage

Beak - bill or rostrum

beak trimming - the partial removal of the beak

Belly - the area beneath the chest of a bird

Billing - a tendency of mated pairs that strengthen couple bonding

bird banding - a tag attached to the leg of a bird to enable identification

bird strike - bird/s that impact with planes in flight

Body down - soft, down feathers underneath a birds outer feathers.

Breast - body part between throat and belly

breeding plumage - plumage displayed by birds during breeding season

Brood - offspring birds

brood patch - an area of bare skin well supplied with blood vessels at the surface, and facilitates the transfer of heat to the eggs

Call - bird vocalization intending to serve as warning alarm

Cloaca - birds expel waste from it; other mate by joining cloaca; females lay eggs from this region

contact call - to make known to their kind the location of a bird

Crissum - feathered area between the vent and the tail

cryptic plumage - plumage meant to camouflage birds

definitive plumage - plumage completely developed and fixed

Down - the softest of the birds feathers

Egg - where birds develop until hatched

egg incubation - act of warming the eggs to promote hatching

Eye-ring - visible ring of feathers surrounding a bird's eyes

Feather - distinct outer "garment" covering a birds' body

feather pecking - a behavioural problem when one bird repeatedly pecks at the feathers of another bird

Fledge - a young bird that completely develops its wing muscles and feather suitable for flight

Fledgling - the period when a completely formed young bird ventures out of the nest and learns to take flight

Flight - the act of soaring in the air with the use of wings

Gizzard - specialized stomach organ found in the digestive tract of some birds used to grind up food and aided with grit or stone particles

Gleaning - a bird strategy used to catch insect prey

Grooming - the act of preening and self-cleaning

Iris - coloured outer ring surrounding birds' pupil

Lek - male aggression when in competition for the attention of a female

Mantle - front area of a bird's upper portion found between nape and top back

Migration - seasonal movement of birds

Morph - a polymorphic plumage colour variance between the same species

Moult - a periodic shedding and replacement of feathers

Nail - hard tissue at the tip of a bird's beak

Nares - two holes leading to the nasal cavities in the bird's skull

Nest - a bird's lair and home; where a female lays eggs and roosts

Over-brooding - a phenomenon when birds continue to brood eggs not likely to hatch

Passerine - any bird of the order Passeriformes

Pinioning - the removal of the joint of a bird's wing farthest from the body preventing flight

Plumage - refers to feathers covering a bird as well as pattern, colour and arrangement of feathers

Plumeology - the study of feathers

pre-alternate moult - also known as the prenuptial moult when basic plumage is shed to make way for nuptial plumage

prebasic moult - moult birds go through after breeding season

Precocial - young birds that after hatched has their eyes open

Preening - grooming od feathers in birds

Quill - the main stem of a feather where all structures branch from

Resident - a non-migratory bird

rictal bristles stiff, tapering feathers around the eyes of some birds

Rosette - a found at the corners of the beaks of some birds. A fleshy rosette area

Rump - area of a bird's body between the end of the back and the base of the tail

sexual dimorphism - common occurrence amongst birds in which males and females of a similar sort display different character traits

Song - bird vocalization associated with courtship

Speculum - A patch of typically bright coloured feathers, often iridescent

Sternum - bird's breastbone

Syrinx - the vocal organs of birds

Tail streamers - narrow tips of the tail of some birds

Talon - claw of bird of prey

Teleoptiles - feathers of an adult bird

Throat - body area located between the chin and the upper part of the breast

Thigh - body part between knee and trunk of the bird's body

Vent - the outer opening of the cloaca

Wings - The bird's forelimbs that are the essential to flight

Wingspan - distance between wings from one wing tip to the other

Photo Credits

Page 1 Photo by user Steve Wilson via Flickr.com,

https://www.flickr.com/photos/pokerbrit/36240224652/

Page 7 Photo by user luckyno3 via Flickr.com,

https://www.flickr.com/photos/luckyno3/3767889095/

Page 18 Photo by user Annette Seifart via Flickr.com,

https://www.flickr.com/photos/aseifart/10517082623/

Page 42 Photo by user Thanate Tan via Flickr.com,

https://www.flickr.com/photos/thanate_tan/16773229705/

Page 67 Photo by user Seabamirum via Flickr.com,

https://www.flickr.com/photos/seabamirum/5490355440/

Page 76 Photo by user Thanate Tan via Flickr.com,

https://www.flickr.com/photos/thanate_tan/16150943994/

Page 88 Photo by user Nik Borrow via Flickr.com,

https://www.flickr.com/photos/128578170@N06/34512376145/

Page 94 Photo by user Andrew-M-Whitman via Flickr.com,

https://www.flickr.com/photos/23967095@N00/6908787434/

References

All About Lovebirds - Animal-world.com

http://animal-world.com/encyclo/birds/lovebirds/LovebirdProfile.htm

Bird Care Guide: Lovebirds - Mspca.org

https://www.mspca.org/pet_resources/bird-care-guide-lovebirds/

Facts About Lovebirds - TheSpruce.com

https://www.thespruce.com/facts-about-lovebirds-390823

How to Tame Your Pet Lovebirds - Birdtrader.co.uk

https://www.birdtrader.co.uk/passerine-advice/how-to-tame-your-pet-lovebirds/399

Lovebirds - TheSpruce.com

https://www.thespruce.com/lovebirds-1236921

Lovebirds: Detailed Information & Photos - Beautyofbirds.com

https://www.beautyofbirds.com/lovebirdinfo.htm

The Complete Step by Step Guide for Beginners - TrainedParrot.com

http://trainedparrot.com/Taming/

www.ingramcontent.com/pod-product-compliance
Lightning Source LLC
Chambersburg PA
CBHW060844050426
42453CB00008B/823